The Precious Things

- To immortalize oneself on earth requires a great deed, drown your deeds in the arrows of greatness. -

Abhijeet Manu

ISBN 978-93-5667-291-8
© Abhijeet Manu 2022
Published in India 2022 by Pencil

A brand of
One Point Six Technologies Pvt. Ltd.
123, Building J2, Shram Seva Premises,
Wadala Truck Terminal, Wadala (E)
Mumbai 400037, Maharashtra, INDIA
E connect@thepencilapp.com
W www.thepencilapp.com

Author biography

Abhijeet Manu is a rising music producer/artist from India. also known as "Elektro Abhiijeet Manu". He comes from a small district of Rajasthan and has a musical background. he has had an interest in music as well as painting and writing since childhood. but the main thing is music. In 2012 he started learning electronic music on his own. He has given some songs internationally as a remix artist. He saw many incidents during the time of lockdown and understood a new truth about life and decided to write a book about his perception" The Precious Things" through this book you will get to know some such knowledge-enhancing things, that can improve your life. Hope you will definitely be able to achieve something from this book he wrote and increase your understanding.

CONTENTS

Preface

This is Abhijeet, also known as the rising Indian music producer **"Elektro Abhiijeet Manu"**. I dedicate this book to **" Lord Maheshwar shiv",** also my mom and elder Sister or author guru. and I also want to say thanks for their love and support. This book I write about this after observing daily incidents in the personal life of the world. so this book gives you a new way of think and some knowledge or wisdom. I only present this book from my perception. I hope you all like it well.

Spiritual Perception - What is Truth

What is the role of a mentor (Guru) in our life-

Who is the Guru, Guru is the one who inspires us to do good deeds in our life. We need a Guru at every turn of life. Because without his guidance we don't get the right path. A guru can be anyone, he can be your spiritual or worldly. The **"Spiritual Guru"** makes you aware of your soul's nature and who you really are. On the contrary, those who are made gurus to achieve the things of the world, help you to achieve your dreams in the world. By the grace of the Guru, we get good intelligence and knowledge of the right path. The path shown by the Guru under challenging circumstances leads us to success. Guru keeps us away from all negative things so always respect your gurus.

- Guru's grace is always with us -2

<u>*What is real freedom in our life-*</u>

what is freedom really? freedom is not being free from someone or something. It can neither be bought nor earned. Because real freedom is from your mind, when you rise above the thoughts and feelings of the mind, then only you will be able to feel this freedom. As thoughts begin to calm down, you will start to know your highest form. This is not possible with thoughts. Because a disturbed person will not be able to do anything. the steadiness of the mind leads to an increase in knowledge.

- Try to grow good seedsin

the plant of the mind -

What exactly is silence-

it's a good thing if you keep quiet through your mouth. But as long as it is good to remain silent where we do not need to speak much because if something goes wrong there will be a need to break the silence. But the process of silence is not complete by not speaking because the human mind keeps on saying something or the other. That's why instead of being silent from above, we should work to remain silent inside. Freeing yourself from thoughts is the first step in surrendering to God.

- Silence is better inside than outside,

nothing better than silence -

<u>*Life is an experience or experience is in life* -</u>

Life is just an experience and we are in that experience as if in a dream. and we're just drifting with the times. We get many things in this life-like memories, happiness, sadness, people, and places. Life is like a train that passes through different platforms. There are some good experiences, some bad, some big, and some small. Many people come to life from those platforms and many leave. This is the same platform known as Circumstances.

- It is better to forget those who

got down on the platform on the train of life -

The biggest healer in our life-

Time is the biggest healer in our life. So according to this, it is not right to be happier in good times and sad in bad times. It can change everything and we don't even know.

That's why we have to move with time and it is better to leave the things which are beyond our understanding or on which we cannot do anything.

*- The ointment is also the ointment of time -*3

Biggest illusion in the world -

The biggest illusion in the world is life and death. But when we are asleep we do not know whether we are alive or not. When we do not know anything but still all the activities of our body are going on smoothly. Cause there's still something that always wakes up. And that is the same soul which is beyond life and death. While surviving in life, we have been sent by God to know the same consciousness.

- Fusion creates an illusion,

take things apart from yourself -

<u>*What does the future say?*</u>-

We all know we can't know what our future holds. So let it be the future. Work only for today but planning for the future is important because the project is a right direction. When we know the address of a place, we reach there automatically. If we make a mistake or fall somewhere, then God gives us the right direction. Because the will of the same God is hidden behind the making of our future projects.

- The future is a divine project,

of course, he does everything right -

Do wishes really come true?-

When we keep any desire in our mind, sometimes we forget it after prayer, that desire definitely appears in front of us in some time. Can't say how long it will take but it will definitely happen and will surprise you. This is the miracle of our subconscious mind. It works for us round the clock even when we are asleep. So pray for your wishes and let it go. Because unknowingly thoughts will come true one day.

- Detachments attracts all things - 4

Jealousy is a Harmful Factor-

If you sometimes feel jealous of someone. which can normally be. So once listen to the beats going on in your body. Because if you understand what we are seeing on the surface everyone's body is different. But we all have one thing in common which is our breathing. If you understand this very deeply, you will find that everyone is the same internally. since then you will not be jealous of anyone. Because the person you're jealous of is none other than you Because everyone's breathing the same So everyone's basically the same and god is inside. So it's self-destructive.

- Jealousy is lousy - 5

Having an opinion about someone without seeing the last outcome-

Don't judge someone without knowing. Because it can make us a partner of sin. Because if later the truth is in our favor, then it is our opinion towards others that will be the cause of our regret. But it does not mean that you trust anyone blindly, because only God knows everyone's mind, we do not have the power to peep into someone's mind. so you have to be patient till the end result.

- Bad opinion for someone can cut

the pinion of your calm mind. -

<u>*comparison or curse-*</u>

To compare yourself with someone means to curse yourself. It also means that you are expressing your disbelief in God, that he made you less than others. But just think that if he has perfected all the parts of your body and sent them to the earth, then who is less than whom here. That's why don't compare yourself by looking at someone's looks, wealth, fame, family, or wealth that, why I didn't get it. Because these things have nothing to do with you, they got after your birth. we are born with only body and breath. So for things that come and go with time, free yourself from the curse of comparison for that.

- Everyone is the same in the eyes of god,

So don't make their blessing a curse from your point of view -

The Dual Identity-

Try to be the same on the inside as we are showing above. Because if we don't do this then our double identity is enough to drown us unnecessarily. because I have seen it in many cases. People meet those with whom they are good but condemn the same person in front of others to whom they are good. this does not mean that all are wrong, this does not apply everywhere, but in most cases, it is so. And somewhere they also give birth to unnecessary controversies.

- If the face is one then

what is the use of dual identity? -

General Perception - How to live better

How should Humans be-

Be the human who mixed with

1.   **(H) -** humble,

2.   **(U) -** unconditional,

3.   **(M) -** magnanimity,

4.   **(A) -** angelic,

5.   **(N) -**naive $=$ _(HUMAN)._

Because if we really have these qualities then this earth will become heaven. And then all the drama will be gone from life, everyone will be happy.

- These five virtues will show

the way to greatness -

Living like a king or giving like a king -

Live like a king and give like a king. it is needed because, By thinking and living like a king, you'll find yourself free from a lot of the little things. then you will love to help others and give support. Because it is also a fact that a person's character is formed according to his thinking. When you will help everyone with this thinking, then you will never get a chance to express regret when people do not help you back.

- A king is capable in every way,

start being like him. -

<u>*Is expectation always painful*</u> -

Expectation is not always painful, if it seems so, then look at your parents and God once. Cause they give you a simple hope that never hurts. And they make it up to you by doing whatever they want. You have to understand who gives you fulfillment. you just do your duty gracefully and expect only from God. And believe me, when you do not keep any expectation from any person or thing, then they will definitely fulfill your every expectation.

- Expectation is a station

on the way to God's grace. -

Choose between true and false-

Have you ever felt like listening to someone's words that who is true and who is a liar? who to trust and whom not. you have to pay attention to that. Because truth and falsehood cannot be identified from the face of any person. If you find someone's point of view reasonable and logical, so you can trust him to some extent. But it is worth noting here that this thing will be applicable only where you come in contact with some philosophical people. In normal day-to-day life, one has to be patient for everything whether it is true or false.

*- The pages of the book of patience
bring forth truth and falsehood. -*

Sisters are gems-

Sisters are precious and priceless. From a sister, we get unconditional love like a mother. There is a sister who makes the house shine like a diamond." **life simplified** "greatly when I realize sister is adorned with the eight great qualities - **G**em, **A**dorable, **R**esponsible, **I**mpeccable, **M**ethodical, **A**ngelic, **D**ivine, **I**deal. It's a humble request to all. respect sisters.

- If we brothers are the lamp of the house,

then sisters are the shining light of that lamp. -

Sanctity of relationships-

If we keep any relationship with anyone in life, then keep it so pure that God himself comes to judge us and he is proud of us. Because today's human beings are trapped in greed and deceit. If all that changes, the earth will become heaven anyway. That's why we should maintain selflessness because real happiness in life will come from that.

- Keep the purity of relationshipslike the purity of fire.-

Why is punctuality important-

You should always reach there on time when going for any urgent work. because time is limited and limited things never wait for anyone. If we are not punctual then time imposes restrictions on us. So be punctual, And then watch the miracle of how much time supports you.

- Make yourself limitless to break the limits of time. -

Above blood relations -

It is not necessary that only blood relations are ours. Everything here is a game of mind's feelings. That's why there are lakhs of people to say, but only one person is better. who can do everything for us. That's why maintaining relationships with your heart.

- Where the mind's string is tied,

there is life even after death. -

<u>Be the precious</u>-

Be a precious diamond for the world. After which, people will remember you for 500 years. it's not as easy as it said. But any great work that you do will make you a priceless diamond in the world. So live life with a great aim and make your name immortal on this earth forever.

- To immortalize oneself on earth requires a great deed,

drown your deeds in the arrows of greatness. -

Notes

Thank you for reading, hope you like the way the author writes and understands. God bless you all, stay connected with abhijeet manu - Facebook / Instagram / Youtube.com / elektroabhiijeetmanu